REGIONS OF AMERICA

THE MIDWEST

Francie Dolan

NorwoodHouse Press

Cataloging-in-Publication Data

Names: Dolan, Francie.
Title: The Midwest / Francie Dolan.
Description: Buffalo, NY : Norwood House Press, 2027. | Series: Regions of America | Includes glossary and index.
Identifiers: ISBN 9781978581197 (pbk.) | ISBN 9781978581203 (library bound) | ISBN 9781978581210 (ebook)
Subjects: LCSH: Middle West--Juvenile literature.
Classification: LCC F351.D65 2027 | DDC 977--dc23

Published in 2027 by
Norwood House Press
2544 Clinton Street
Buffalo, NY 14224

Designer: Rhea Magaro
Editor: Tricia Hoffman

Photo credits: Cover, p. 1 TommyBrison/Shutterstock.com; p. 5 JaySi/Shutterstock.com; p. 6 Georgi Baird/Shutterstock.com; p. 7 Nagel Photography/Shutterstock.com; p. 8 Evgenii Bakhchev/Shutterstock.com; p. 11 John Gress Media Inc/Shutterstock.com; p. 12 Library of Congress; p. 13 Library of Congress/P&P; p. 14 Eddie J. Rodriquez/Shutterstock.com; p. 15 James Andrews1/Shutterstock.com; p. 17 photo.ua/Shutterstock.com; p. 18 Robert R French/Shutterstock.com; p. 21 colcatkan/Shutterstock.com;

Printed in the United States of America

Some of the images in this book illustrate individuals who are models. The depictions do not imply actual situations or events.

CPSIA compliance information: Batch #CSNHP27: For further information contact Norwood House Press at 1-800-237-9932.

TABLE OF CONTENTS

WHERE IS THE MIDWEST?

The Midwest is a **region** of the United States. It has 12 states.

The Midwest

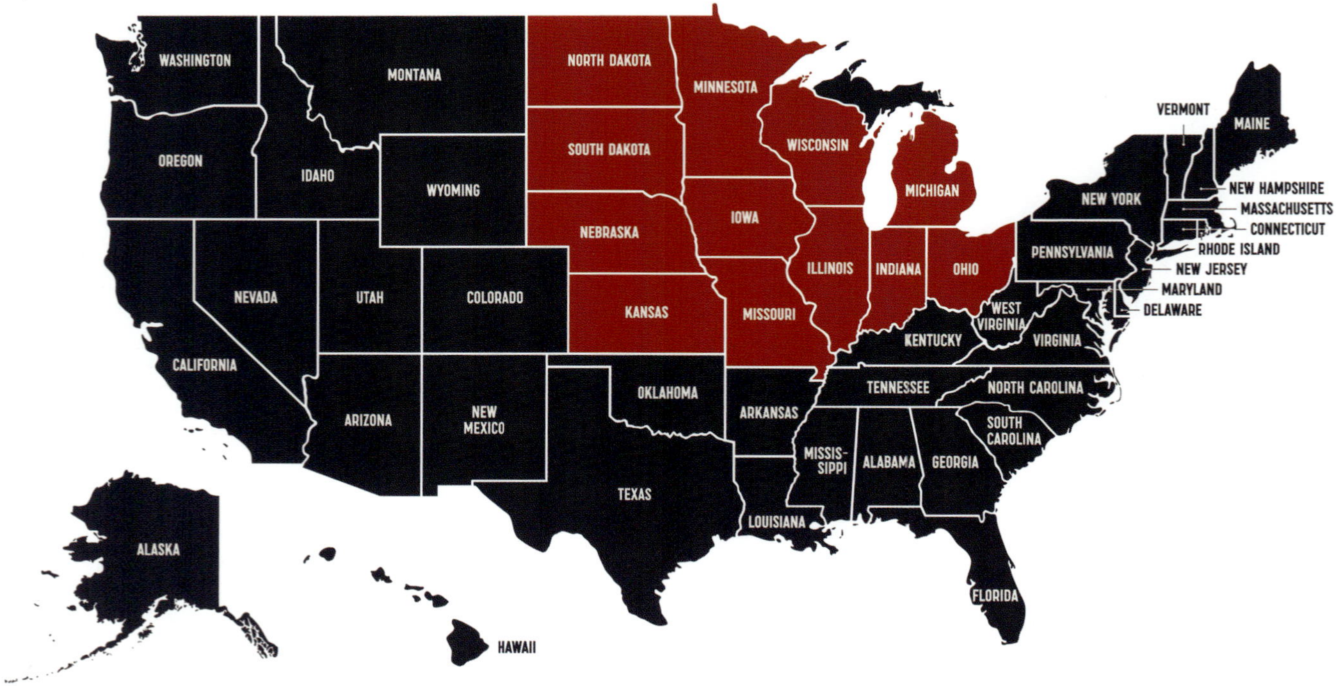

THE LAND

The Midwest is in the middle of the country. It is sometimes called "America's Heartland."

There are four **distinct** seasons. Summers are warm, and winters are cold.

Thousands of years ago, **glaciers** pushed down on the land. They made it flat. There are few hills or mountains.

When the glaciers melted, they left **minerals** behind. This makes the soil good for farming.

The Great Plains are grasslands that stretch across some of the Midwest. Most of America's **grain** is grown here on huge farms.

The five Great Lakes formed when the glaciers melted. These vast lakes have about one-fifth of Earth's fresh water.

Many **factories** are built near the Great Lakes. Detroit, Michigan, has lots of car factories. It is called the "auto capital of the world."

THE PEOPLE

Indigenous people once lived across the Midwest. Some tribes were the Ojibwe, Hidatsa, and Sioux.

Many families came from Europe. They came from Germany, England, and other countries.

Others came to the Midwest to work on farms or in factories.

Some Midwesterners live in **rural** areas.
They live in small towns.

Other Midwesterners live in cities. Chicago, Illinois, is the third largest city in America.

THINGS TO SEE AND DO

You can ride a **tram** inside the Gateway Arch. It is in St. Louis, Missouri. From the top, you can look down on the Mississippi River.

You can marvel at Mount Rushmore. It is in South Dakota. The **monument** has the faces of four American presidents carved into a mountain.

You can play at Sleeping Bear Dunes. It is a park in Michigan. After sliding down giant piles of sand, cool off by jumping into Lake Michigan!

GLOSSARY

distinct (di-STINGKT): different from the rest; easy to tell apart from others

factories (FAK-tur-eez): buildings where products are made in large numbers

glaciers (GLAY-shurs): giant, slow-moving masses of ice

grain (grayn): the seeds of wheat, oats, and other plants that are used to make cereal, bread, and other foods

Indigenous (in-DI-juh-nuhs): the earliest known people to live in a place

minerals (MIN-ur-uhlz): solids that form naturally in Earth and that do not come from an animal or plant; calcium and iron are examples of minerals

monument (MAHN-yuh-muhnt): a statue, building, or other structure built to remind people of important people and events